Through Ups and Downs of Life

Poems that echo faith, fate, and freedom

RAJESH SHARMA

INDIA · SINGAPORE · MALAYSIA

ISBN

Hardcase 979-8-89929-937-7
Paperback 979-8-89906-313-8

Table of Contents

Table of Contents

Foreword

Poetry has always been a mirror to the soul, reflecting our deepest emotions, struggles, and triumphs. *Through Ups and Downs of Life* is a collection of poems that weave together themes of fate, love, loss, resilience, and the inevitable march of time. The poet masterfully crafts each piece with a rich tapestry of words, inviting readers into a realm of introspection and wonder. This collection is not just a book of verses; it is an experience—one that lingers in the mind long after the final page is turned.

Preface

Every poem in this collection carries a piece of life—some drawn from personal experiences, others inspired by the stories of those around us. Poetry has the power to transcend time and space, speaking to the human condition in ways that prose often cannot. Through these verses, I hope to take you on a journey that touches your heart and stirs your thoughts. May these words resonate with you, as they have with me in their creation.

Acknowledgements

This book is dedicated to my beloved father and mother, who are no longer in this world but continue to live in my heart. My father, a passionate footballer, taught me the spirit of sportsmanship, while my mother, a Hindi teacher, unknowingly nurtured my love for poetry and literature. They gifted me a childhood filled with warmth, freedom, and the space to explore life on my own terms.

I extend my heartfelt gratitude to:

Every friend, foe, and acquaintance—each of you has played a role in shaping my journey, whether through moments of kindness or lessons learned in adversity.

My pet dog, Newton, who, with his unconditional love, taught me the true meaning of companionship and compassion.

My students, from tiny toddlers to inquisitive pre-teens, who have helped me rediscover the world through their innocent wonder and boundless curiosity.

The silent helpers—digital tools—that lent a hand with images, words, and rhymes when I called on them.

To all who have touched my life in ways big and small—this book, in some way, belongs to you too.

Introduction to the Poems

This collection brings together 21 carefully crafted poems, each exploring different facets of life. From quiet acts of heroism in everyday life, as depicted in *The Mountain Man*, to the bittersweet nostalgia of *The Wilted Garden*, the poems traverse a wide emotional spectrum. Love, loss, hope, and destiny intertwine, creating a poetic mosaic that speaks to the soul. *The Last Game of Hide and Seek* offers a tender tribute to a child's unshaken faith amidst loss—a silent echo of sacrifice and love. Whether it is the depth of a mother's love, the silent passage of time, or the wisdom hidden in the whispers of the wind, each poem carries a profound truth waiting to be discovered.

Poem Compilation

Section 1: Faith and Divine Whispers

Friend in Prayer

When words fall short, and hearts are sore,
A silent prayer is worth much more.
No voice is raised, no sound is heard,
Yet faith is strong in whispered word.

A Silent Bond

We speak in silence, soul to soul,
A quiet love that makes us whole.
No need for voices, loud or grand,
Just trust, like footprints in the sand.

A Cry for Mercy

Tears that glisten in the night,
Hearts weighed down in endless fight.
A plea, a cry, a whispered call,
To He who listens, He who knows all.

Whispers to the Divine

A prayer at dawn, a wish at dusk,
Hope lingers in the air like musk.
A whisper sent to skies above,
Carrying faith, carrying love.

Who Will You Call Pure, O God?

Not robes nor rituals, gold nor name,
Define the soul or cleanse the shame.
A heart that loves, a hand that gives,
That is where true virtue lives.

Section 2: Fate, Loss, and Resilience

The Line That Changed It All

One step, one word, one moment small,
Yet it rewrote the tale of all.
A path once straight, now bent and curled,
Fate's hand reshaping all the world.

The Fragile Thread

Life's thread is thin, yet holds so tight,
A gentle pull, a twist of might.
We walk on edges, soft yet steep,
Holding to dreams we long to keep.

If Flowers Could Speak

Would they whisper tales of old?
Of love once warm, now lost and cold?
Or bloom anew in hopeful air,
Shedding sorrow, growing fair?

The Last Game of Hide and Seek

Shadows fall where laughter played,
Echoes lost in time's cascade.
One last count, one final chase,
Memories fade, but leave a trace.

The Wilted Garden

Leaves once bright, now brown and dry,
Beneath a tired, endless sky.
Yet even wilted roots can hold,
A strength unseen, a tale untold.

Section 3: Life's Journeys and Lessons

A Place Called Heavell

A land between the high and low,
Where sinners dream and saints may go.
No judgment reigns, no price to pay,
Just second chances every day.

A Journey to Motherhood

A heartbeat whispers, small and new,
A bond unbroken, strong and true.
The path is long, yet love will guide,
A mother's arms, a child's pride.

Of Books, Boots, and Dentures Lost

A tale of things both old and new,
Of misplaced joys and sorrows too.
Not all that's lost is lost for long,
Some find their way where hearts belong.

The Lost Traveller

A path once clear, now fades in mist,
A journey lost, a fate dismissed.
Yet every road, though veiled and blind,
May lead to what one seeks to find.

The Wisdom of Choosing Battles

Not every fight is worth the pain,
Not every loss is truly vain.
To rise above, to step aside,
Is sometimes where true victors hide.

Section 4: Love, Freedom, and Humanity

Of Dogs and Men

Loyal hearts and fearless eyes,
Lessons taught 'neath open skies.
Not all who speak have love so true,
Not all who bark are threats to you.

Let Them Be Free

A cage of gold, a lock so tight,
Can never match the boundless flight.
Let dreams take wing, let voices soar,
For love should chain the heart no more.

The Mountain Man

Stone by stone, a dream was laid,
A path through rock his hands had made.
No wealth, no fame, no grand design,
Just love that built a road divine.

Love's Laughter

Not every love is soft and sweet,
Some dance in fire, some skip a beat.
Yet in its chaos, wild and bright,
Love's laughter makes the world feel light.

A Place Beyond Walls

No flags, no names, no rigid lines,
Just hearts that meet, just hands that bind.
A world unchained, so vast, so wide,
Where love and hope walk side by side.

Beyond Fear, Beyond Faith

When fear dissolves and faith stands tall,
The chains of doubt begin to fall.
Not faith alone, nor courage blind,
But love that leads the heart and mind.

Section 1
Faith and Divine Whispers

Each morning, paths cross, yet words remain unspoken.
A silent bond between the burdened and the blessed,
A whispered prayer for a stranger's struggle—
A hope that life grants him the peace he deserves.

A Friend in Prayer

Every morning as I walk by,
I see your toil, your silent sigh.
A cycle laden with dreams and strife,
Your eyes hold hope, carving out life.

And in the night, I meet you again,
Returning home through fatigue and pain.
The battles of the day etched on your face,
Yet your smile still holds a quiet grace.

I reflect on my life, so at ease,
With meals, rest, and moments of peace.
But your journey, filled with endless fight,
Moves my soul and humbles my might.

Oh, stranger, your story I see,
Reminds me of struggles once faced by me.
When my own feet bore the weight of dreams,
And my days were stitched with silent screams.

Dear God, I bow my head in prayer,
As You've lifted my burdens with care.
Do the same for this tireless soul,
And make their life a little more whole.

At times, I wish to stop and say,
"Friend, you're not alone in this fray.

Your relentless fight, your endless pain,
Resounds in hearts again and again."

But I stay silent, each time I pass,
For my prayer is pure, and words may trespass.
Let this unspoken wish in the air remain,
A hope to ease your toil and pain.

For you, I send a heartfelt plea,
That your efforts bloom abundantly.
May joy embrace you, sorrow depart,
And peace find its way into your heart.

Through the years of boundless joy and silent sorrows,
two souls walk together, hearts entwined.
But as time bends their journey, one question lingers—
Who will remain when the other fades?

A Silent Bond

From a tiny pup, just thirty-five days,
To twelve long years of countless ways,
You've shown me love, pure and true,
A gift of life I owe to you.

In your infancy, I saw tender grace,
Wide-eyed wonder in your furry face.
Through childhood days, so playful, so free,
You taught the joy of simplicity to me.

In adolescence, with spirit untamed,
Boundless energy, yet never blamed.
Through youthful years, your strength inspired,
A loyal heart, never tired.

And now, as age softens your frame,
Your love remains steady, still the same.
You teach me courage to face the end,
As life's full circle begins to bend.

Though I fear not what death may bring,
One thought leaves my heart a sting—
Who will hold you, my dearest friend,
When my own journey comes to an end?

When I'm gone, and they bring me home,
Let no one deny your rightful roam.
Lick my face, your way to grieve,
Your love's language, I still believe.

For in that act, so simple, so pure,
You'll show the bond that will endure.
A love that death can never sever,
My loyal companion, my friend forever.

So, in my final breath, I pray,
May you find peace when I fade away.
For you have been my heart, my guide,
A beacon of love, always by my side.

Silent voices echo through the earth,
mothers torn, lives stolen at birth.
Yet, in the stillness of the fading night,
a plea remains—will mercy find the light?

A Cry for Mercy

A cow's udder flows with love so pure,
For her calf alone, her bond secure.
Yet hands of greed steal her gift,
Turning nurture into a cruel rift.

A hen lays eggs, a mother's right,
To warm them through each tender night.
But shattered shells and stolen dreams,
Feed the world's insatiable schemes.

A goat gives birth, her joy untold,
To watch her kids run free and bold.
Yet blades await, and blood is spilt,
For fleeting taste, a feast of guilt.

A fish, in water, breathes her song,
Where she belongs, where she is strong.
Yet dragged to land, she gasps in vain,
A silent scream, a life in pain.

We call the tiger fierce and wild,
Yet steal the future of her child.
Who is the beast, who spills the red,
Who turns the earth to fields of dread?

Oh, mankind, when will you see,
That mercy is the only key?
To let them live, to let them be,
To break the chains and set them free.

God, will there be a time so bright,
Where love outshines the hunter's might?
Where every life, both great and small,
Is treated fair, is loved by all?

Beneath the vast, silent sky, an old man sits—his heart heavy with unanswered prayers, his eyes searching the heavens for whispers long unheard. Will the stars unveil the truth, or will silence be his only reply?

Whispers to the Divine

They call me wise, for the years I've seen,
For the silver strands where black had been.
Yet in my heart, a tempest sways,
With questions deep that cloud my days.

If God's our Father, kind and just,
Why then this world of sand and dust?
Some are born to wealth and grace,
While others toil in a cruel embrace.

Some minds shine like morning light,
While others struggle through endless night.
Some hands paint with magic untold,
While some remain weak, never to hold.

Beauty blesses some like springtime's song,
While others walk where shadows throng.
If all are His, if love is true,
Why does life weave joy and rue?

And then, the ones I cherished most,
For whom my heart was proud to boast,
Left behind but tears and pain,
Like vanishing footprints in the rain.

Yet some, to whom I gave no claim,
Stood by me in joy and shame.
Why does kindness bloom in ways unknown,
From hands unheld, in love unshown?

Oh, how I longed to give in kind,
To those who blessed my heart and mind!
Yet fate stood firm, denied my plea,
Left me bound, unworthy, free.

So tell me, Lord, in endless space,
Why did You weave this tangled maze?
Why not a world so pure, so bright,
Where wrong is dust and all is right?

But silence reigns, no voice replies,
The stars just glimmer in distant skies.
Perhaps the answers hide unseen,
Beyond the veil, where souls convene.

Till then, I walk with wondering eyes,
Counting stars in moonlit skies,
Carrying questions yet unsaid,
With whispers sent where angels tread.

Who is truly pure? A humble shopkeeper, a devoted schoolmaster, a scientist striving for change, and a dancer moving to survive— each walks a different path, yet each carries truth in their heart. But while they toil in quiet dignity, those who preach virtue often hide deception behind sacred robes. **If purity is measured by conscience, not title, then who will God call pure?**

Who Will You Call Pure, O God?

I know a shopkeeper in a nameless town,
With a creaking shutter and a life worn down.
Sells soap, salt, and rice with steady hands,
Counts no blessings, makes no grand stands.
Cash only, fair price — no deceit, no flair,
Just a common man, breathing honest air.

I know a master with chalk-dusted palms,
Whose voice wraps children like lullaby psalms.
His joy is their joy, his pride is their flight,
Each lesson a prayer, each success — pure light.
He boasts not of wealth, nor of fame or caste,
His riches are stories of students who passed.

I know a scientist, wild-eyed and worn,
Whose family feels both love and scorn.
He builds a tool to cleanse the drains,
To free hands from filth, from sewage stains.
Called crazy by neighbours, misunderstood by kin,
But his conscience is clear — he knows no sin.

I know a dancer, beneath neon skies,
Where morals melt and judgement lies.
She sways for survival, her dignity torn,

A mother, a daughter, in silence reborn.
Every rupee earned in her weary hand,
Is cleaner than gold washed in holy sand.

I know a pandit, draped in saffron pride,
His smile a mask, his greed can't hide.
He trades salvation for coins and gems,
Makes rituals prisons, and prayers condemned.
Sandalwood scents can't cleanse his schemes,
Yet he walks revered — a god in men's dreams.

I know a maulvi, sharp-eyed and stern,
Preaching fire where love should burn.
His sermons drip with poison and fear,
Whispers of 'jihad' to the young and clear.
Yet his gaze strays where it shouldn't go,
Piety worn thin, like a staged shadow show.

I know a priest in robe of white,
With cross that glints in candlelight.
He speaks of virtue, of sin and grace,
Yet lust leaks from his holy face.
Behind the veil of confessions heard,
Lie secrets too dark to put into word.

O God, I ask with trembling heart,
Why do the pure live lives torn apart?
Why do the wolves wear robes so fine,
While the lambs are left with scraps of time?
Is purity the scent of clean conscience alone,
Or does society bless the crown and the throne?

Who will You call pure, O keeper of skies?
The man with no wealth but truth in his eyes?
The mother who dances to feed and survive?
Or the priests who flourish on fear and lies?

Why do You let the holy be hollow,
While the humble swallow sorrow and follow?
Do You see them, God? Do You even care?
Or have You left earth to rot in despair?

If purity lives in hearts unseen,
Then bless the shopkeeper, modest and clean.
Bless the master with lessons to give,
Bless the dancer who teaches her child to live.
Let the wolves wear crowns if they must,
For truth will rise from honest dust.

For now, I leave my prayer unsaid,
Knowing some truths are born when we're dead.
But still, I ask — my faith worn thin —
Who will You call pure, O God within?

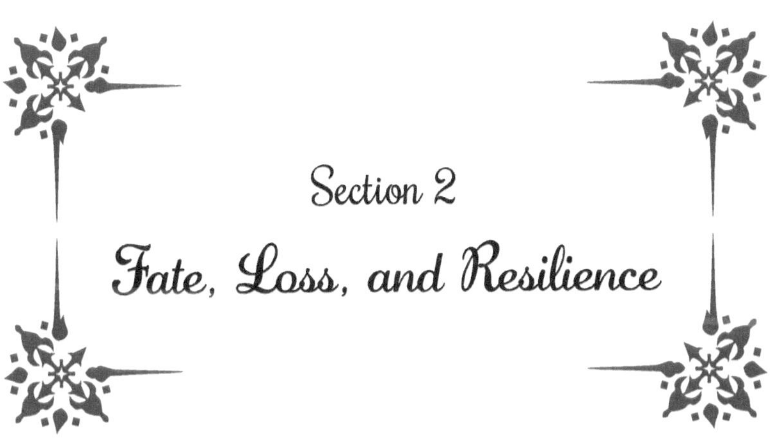

Section 2
Fate, Loss, and Resilience

Born from the echoes of his mother's migration during Partition, the poet captures a nation's sorrow—broken families, lost love, and a land divided by an unforgiving line. Yet, amidst the grief, a dream endures: a world where borders fade and love prevails.

The Line That Changed It All

On 15th August, freedom was won,
Yet sorrow rose with the morning sun.
A line was drawn, a fate was sealed,
A nation wept, its wounds revealed.

The scent of earth, so fresh, so sweet,
Danced with the rain in a rhythmic beat.
Yet hearts lay heavy, torn apart,
Love displaced by maps and charts.

A bride stood still, her eyes turned red,
Her soldier groom with vows unsaid.
He kissed her hand, then walked away,
To guard the line where shadows lay.

A mother wailed, her cries so deep,
Her fallen son now wrapped in sleep.
She held him close, but time stood cold,
His name now carved in letters bold.

The Ravi and Chenab still freely flow,
The winds still whisper, the monsoons still blow.
Yet men once kin now stand apart,
Divided by walls, not by heart.

O Lord, if love still has a say,
Let borders fade, let hate decay.
Let not a line define our fate,
Let love rise up—and conquer hate.

Trust is given like a gentle thread—delicate, full of hope, yet vulnerable to time and betrayal. As bonds fray and silence grows, the weight of loss lingers. But even in brokenness, trust bends like light, finding a way to shine again.

The Fragile Thread

Trust is a fragile, fearless thing —
Offered with hope, like birds in spring.
Soft in its flight, pure in its song,
Yet seldom does it last for long.

He gave his trust — to friend, to kin,
As if the world could hold within
A place where words and hands align,
Where truth and love together shine.

He stepped away to lighten loads,
To clear for others smoother roads.
But quiet exits leave no trace —
The absent soon are out of place.

When paper spoke what hearts concealed,
The ink betrayed what time revealed.
For blood, though thick, can thin with years —
What's left are shadows, doubts, and fears.

He placed his trust in vows and rings,
In quiet homes and simple things.
Each earned coin laid within her hand —
Like offerings made to sacred land.

But hearts can drift like untied boats,
Carried by softer winds and hopes.
What once was shared, now stood apart —
A house of walls, no longer heart.

Yet blame and rage were not his way,
For trust itself had paved the day.
Betrayal comes not from the foe —
Only from hands once held below.

And still, despite the weight of years,
The loss, the quiet, hidden tears —
He trusts the sun will rise once more,
That love may knock on some new door.

For trust, though broken, bends like light,
It finds a crack, however slight.
And through that crack, life still may grow —
A softer trust, more wise, less show.

Flowers bloom not to be taken, but to dance with the wind and kiss the sun. Their petals hold whispers of life, their roots cradle hope. To pluck them is to silence their story—yet in their freedom, all earth's magic unfolds.

If Flowers Could Speak

If flowers could speak, what would they say,
To hands that reach, to hearts that sway?
Would they whisper soft, or cry aloud,
As fingers tear them from their cloud?

"I bloom not to wilt in your vase,
Nor to brighten your fleeting gaze.
I dance with the breeze, I drink from the sun,
My life's own story has just begun."

You pluck me for temples, for love, for show,
But in your joy, my sorrow grows.
I feed the bees, I call the sky,
I give the earth my sweetest sigh.

Each petal holds a drop of light,
A secret song, a wing in flight.
I cradle life within my stem,
I am the hope of seeds to them.

"With every tug, a future falls,
A forest lost, a hush in calls.
For what is beauty if not free—
A flower chained is misery."

Let me bloom where I belong,
In earth's warm arms, where roots grow strong.
Not caged in glass, or bound by thread,
But kissed by dawn, not left for dead.

So if you love me, let me be,
A gift for all— the sky, the bee.
Let beauty live and not be sold,
For life is more than fleeting gold.

"Pluck me not, dear child so bright,
For I hold dreams in morning light.
Let me shimmer, sway, and grow,
And all earth's magic I will show."

A little boy waits at the gate, eyes full of hope, arms ready for an embrace that never comes. His mother, a frontline doctor in the **2020 pandemic**, fought bravely—until the battle claimed her. Too young to understand loss, he believes she's still playing their favourite game, hiding just beyond reach.

But some games never end.

"The Last Game of Hide and Seek" is a hauntingly tender tribute to love, sacrifice, and a child's unshaken faith in a reunion that will never be.

The Last Game of Hide and Seek

A little child of just three, so sweet, so small,
Every morning he'd watch, standing proud and tall.
His mommy in her white coat, off to work she'd go,
With love in her eyes, and a gentle glow.

Each evening at the gate, he would stand and wait,
Mommy's car would stop — his joy couldn't wait.
She'd rush to him fast, scoop him in her embrace,
Covering him in kisses, all over his face.

Then came daddy too, with laughter and cheer,
Playing hide and seek, chasing ball so near.
These were their moments, so precious, so bright,
Their small perfect world, wrapped in soft light.

With dreams of tomorrow, toys lined up in a row,
He'd drift into sleep, with a teddy in tow.
And mommy, in silence, would dream even more,
Of a shining future for the child she adored.

But one such morning, like any before,
Mommy's coat was white, standing near the door.
"Biggest teddy, don't forget!" the child did say,
"Yes baby, love you — I'll bring it today."

Evening came, the child stood at the gate,
But mommy rushed inside — something didn't wait.
Daddy held him back, "No, not just yet."
Confused little eyes, with tears now wet.

"Finish your milk, then we'll go," daddy said,
The child obeyed, though his heart felt dread.
He ran to his room, quiet and slow,
Gulped his milk down, hoping soon they'd go.

"Daddy, let's go, I want to play with her now."
Daddy smiled, hiding grief somehow.
"Tonight, let's play hide and seek instead,
You knock the door, and she'll hide," he said.

The boy knocked, laughter filled the air,
From inside came sounds of a playful scare —
"Meow-meow," then "woof-woof" echoed out loud,
Cheerful tricks to make her child proud.

Each night the game would start anew,
Yet something felt missing — the child knew.
His innocent heart sensed what none could explain,
A silent storm, a hidden pain.

"No more hide and seek," he finally said,
Tears unspoken, fears unsaid.
"I want to see mommy, no more games,
Let's end this hiding, I'm tired of shame."

The house grew quiet, the air turned still,
A silence crept in, heavy and chill.

On a plate lay petals, soft and bright,
Four strangers stood, eyes glistening with light.
The boy ran to daddy, "Where is she?"
He pointed to a photo — "Here's mommy."

Trembling hands took petals in small grip,
Placed them near the photo, lips quivering, stiff.
"No hide and seek? No running today?"
Daddy's silence had nothing to say.

A siren wailed, the procession began,
Cars followed slow, like a mourning caravan.
At the cremation ground, they stood apart,
The boy, the daddy, and a shattered heart.

Wrapped in white, from head to toe,
Mommy lay still, in a gentle glow.
Flames rose high, tears ran free,
The child still hoped — maybe she'll see.

With trembling hope, and a tear-stained face,
He whispered to the sky — "One last embrace."
And somewhere above, in the soft golden light,
A mother kissed her son goodnight.

Once, a garden thrived under the tender hands of its devoted keeper. He toiled, he nurtured, he loved—until the very blossoms he cherished chose to drift away, seeking grander horizons. Now, amidst the empty flowerbed and the silence of fallen petals, he stands alone, his hands still longing to give, his heart still whispering their names.

But does love ever truly fade, or does it wait—like a garden yearning for the return of spring?

"Wilted Garden" is a hauntingly beautiful tale of love, loss, and the quiet ache of being forgotten.

Wilted Garden

Once bloomed a garden, lush and bright,
With petals bathed in golden light.
At dawn, the birds would come and sing,
Soft melodies on feathered wings.

Within its heart, a flowerbed lay,
Two tender buds in gentle sway.
The gardener, with devoted care,
Would nurture them with love so rare.

With sweat and toil, he fed the ground,
His aching hands, with duty bound.
The soil drank deep his silent pain,
As he shielded them from storm and rain.

The flowerbed would proudly say,
"My blossoms shine in grand display!
They are my world, my joy, my pride,
Who else would love them, stand beside?"

And hearing this, the buds would glow,
Their hearts convinced, they'd never go.
In petals wrapped, they found their grace,
A shelter safe, a warm embrace.

The seasons turned, the buds unfurled,
Their fragrance spread across the world.
The little garden, once so wide,
Now felt too small to house their pride.

The flowerbed began to dream,
Of riches vast, of grander schemes.
The singing birds, the gentle breeze,
No longer could its heart appease.

The garden walls, the rooted trees,
Became a burden, not a peace.
The gardener's hands, once firm and wise,
Were seen with scorn in judgment's eyes.

"This soil is barren, old, and weak,
No nourishment for us to seek.
The gardener, crude, unfit to tend,
His hands are rough, his ways must end.

His sweat repels, his labour stains,
His love is shackles, forged in chains.
No flowers thrive in such a place,
We must escape, embrace our fate!"

The gardener watched in silent ache,
As roots were torn, as hearts would break.
He stood alone, arms open wide,
Yet none looked back, none turned inside.

Then came a storm, fierce and wild,
It crushed the bed, the earth defiled.
The garden wept, the flowers cried,
Yet in the wind, their whispers died.

And there he knelt in hollow land,
Dust and sorrow on his hands.
No tears were left, no words to say,
Only memories swept away.

With empty eyes, he tilled the ground,
Not blood, nor sweat—just grief profound.
And so he tended barren earth,
A wilted garden, lost its worth.

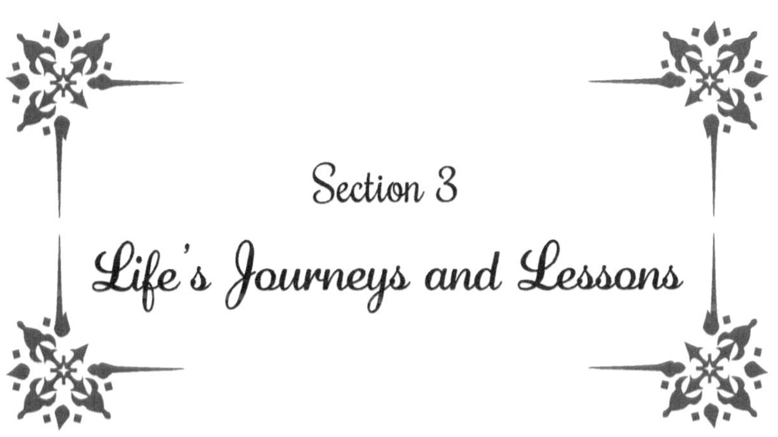

Section 3
Life's Journeys and Lessons

Not quite heaven, not quite hell—just a place for those who walked both light and shadow. A life well-lived, mistakes well-paid, and a heart that still dares to dream. *A Place Called Heavell* is a journey of acceptance, where imperfect souls find a home beyond judgment, in a land of toil, love, and rest.

A Place Called Heavell

As a boy, so full of glee,
Dreams as vast as the endless sea.
Friends who cheered, a heart so light,
A world that shimmered, bold and bright.

With fire inside, I chased the stars,
Through winding roads and battle scars.
Tasted triumph, knew defeat,
Hope still danced, though oft discreet.

I questioned fate, I questioned time,
Why luck felt like a fleeting chime.
Yet now I stand, and finally see,
Life gave enough—it gave to me.

A roof, a meal, my daily bread,
No debts to haunt, no fear to dread.
Though silver lines now grace my hair,
The hills still call, the roads still dare.

I walked in light, I strayed in shade,
A soul of both—well-earned, well-paid.
Not pure enough for heaven's gate,
Yet not for hell's eternal fate.

So, Lord, I ask, when I depart,
Let me rest where real souls start—
A land of toil, of love, of rest,
Where imperfect hearts are still blessed.

Not quite heaven, not quite hell,
A home for men like me—**Heavell.**

From a cherished daughter to a determined dreamer, and finally, to a mother—this is the journey of a woman who finds her truest self in the embrace of her child.

The Journey to Motherhood

Once a child, so bright, so sweet,
Mom and Dad's joy, their world complete.
Princess, darling, a beauty so rare,
Basking in love, floating on air.

At school, they called me wise and keen,
A radiant smile, a mind so serene.
Praise and glory, medals in hand,
Proudly I walked, life seemed so grand.

Years went by, my beauty grew,
Eyes that followed, hearts I knew.
Names they whispered, longing gaze,
A fleeting thrill, a golden phase.

With books and dreams, I carved my way,
A job so grand, a handsome pay.
Yet in my heart, a whisper stayed,
A hollow space, a light that swayed.

And then it came, the moment divine,
A life within, a spark so fine.
Not wealth, nor fame, nor fleeting praise,
Could match the love that filled my days.

A tiny hand, a heartbeat near,
Softest breath, so pure, so dear.
No greater joy, no prouder stand,
Than holding life in my own hand.

For now, I know, through joy and strife,
A mother's love is the crown of life.
Thank you, God, for this sacred role,
For motherhood has made me whole.

Through the playful chaos of youth and the quirks of aging, this poem takes you on a journey where books took a backseat to football, glasses are misplaced in plain sight, and forgotten dentures turn a feast into an unexpected adventure. A lighthearted yet poignant reflection on the passage of time, it reminds us that while the years may change our pace, they never dull our spirit.

Of Books, Boots, and Dentures Lost

In school days, my bag lay light,
Books forgotten, out of sight.
Not careless, but a heart that knew,
Football gear was all that grew.

Shoes and stockings, caps for knees,
Packed with care, with perfect ease.
Timetable slipped like grains of sand,
But my football kit — always at hand.

Years rolled on, now glasses worn,
Middle-aged and slightly torn.
Tea and rusk, my morning grace,
But glasses lost — what a chase!

I searched the table, floor, and chair,
Desperate fingers combed the air.
Until I caught, with quiet surprise,
A headline clear before my eyes.

They perched already on my nose,
The same old pair — my daily dose.
Not as bad as what came next,
A party night, I was perplexed.

Foodie heart, so full of cheer,
Till halfway there — oh dear, oh dear!
My dentures sat at home, forgot,
What could I eat? — not quite a lot.

Soft rasgullas, creamy dahi,
Kheer and halwa came to rescue me.
Paratha torn in tiny bits,
Saved the evening, piece by piece.

Someday soon, I know I'll need,
A walking stick — my future steed.
But that, I'm sure, I'll not forget,
None who needs one ever yet.

And when my time has come to rest,
I'll call on four old friends, my best.
Their shoulders firm, their steps so slow,
Will gently guide me where I must go.

Through mist-laden paths and fading dreams, a wanderer treads—his purpose forgotten, his compass lost. Yet, within the shadows of uncertainty, a whisper calls him forward. Will he find his way again?

The Lost Traveller

On twisted paths and tangled ways,
Through mazes dark and foggy haze;
A wandering soul, lost and lone,
Somewhere, his purpose — long outgrown.

Struggles outside and storms within,
Clouded his heart, his vision dim;
The compass broke, the map unclear,
He walked for miles — yet nowhere near.

Dreams once bright now torn apart,
The weight of life pressed on his heart;
Each step unsure, each breath a sigh,
Beneath the vast, unending sky.

But deep within, a spark survived,
A whisper said — you are alive;
Fill your heart with hope anew,
Paint the world in brighter hue.

With courage bold and spirit high,
He faced the sun, the open sky;
To weave a life from dreams once frayed,
He walked again — unafraid.

"Not all battles are meant to be fought, and not all victories bring triumph. Through wisdom, patience, and discernment, one learns the true art of choosing when to stand firm and when to let go. This poem explores the delicate balance between conflict and peace, reminding us that sometimes, the greatest strength lies in restraint."

The Wisdom of Choosing Battles

In the dance of life, we often face
The trials that come with a bitter grace,
Where fights arise, and words may sting,
Yet wisdom whispers what it might bring.

Fight not when doubt clouds your heart,
When you're unsure if you play your part,
The truth may seem in your own sight,
But others, too, may carry light.

Give room for thought, the other view,
For every story has its hue.
The mind may stray, the eyes may deceive,
In kindness, let the truth reprieve.

And when your foe is weak in might,
Victory is hollow, lacking light.
A barren land where no one stands,
A flag unfurled in empty hands.

Forgiveness, then, is strength to show,
And pray for wisdom to help them grow.
For in the struggle, no pride is won,
When the battle is lost before it's begun.

Lastly, beware the one with naught to lose,
Who has no wealth, no fame to choose.
For in their eyes, the fight is clear—
They'll drag you down without a fear.

So choose your wars with heart and mind,
Let peace and wisdom both align.
For *dharma's* path is more than just,
It's knowing when to act with trust.

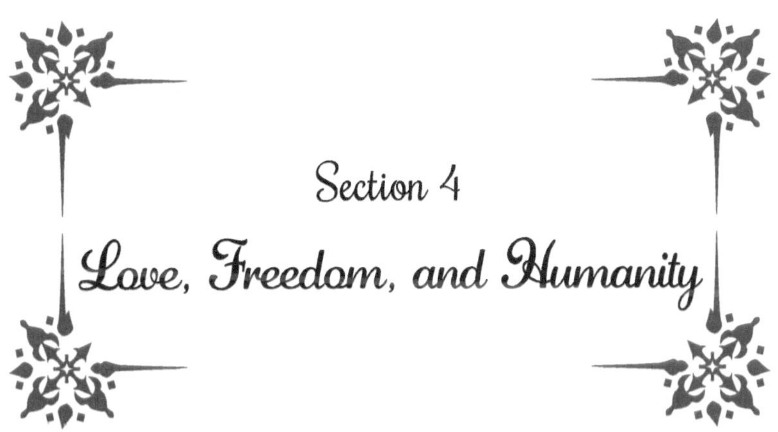

Section 4
Love, Freedom, and Humanity

In a world where loyalty wags its tail and deception wears a smile, trust is measured not in words, but in the honesty of a gaze.

Of Dogs and Men

I walked my pup through streets unknown,
Where elder dogs would bark and groan.
With every step, their teeth would flash,
Their growls like thunder, sharp and brash.

But time, that sculptor, shaped my pup,
He grew in size, he stood grown-up.
The same old pack still barked and howled,
But from afar — no longer proud.

In dogs I saw a simple truth,
A primal code, from age to youth.
They guard their patch, they mark their space,
They fight or yield with honest face.

A wagging tail — a sign so clear,
Of friendship true, no need to fear.
A snarl, a growl, a flash of tooth,
Announces anger, plain and smooth.

But men — oh men — a different breed,
With words that lie and hearts that bleed.
They smile and bow, their tails may wag,
Yet hide a dagger in their bag.

They shake your hand with warmth so bright,
While plotting poison in the night.
They crave, they scheme, they play pretend,
Their kindness often has an end.

A dog may bite when anger burns,
But man can smile while taking turns,
To stab, to twist, to lie, to cheat,
And still appear so kind, so sweet.

I trust my dog — his heart is plain,
Through joy, through fear, through love, through pain.
But men, with masks that shift and blend,
Are harder still to call a friend.

Twelve years, a dog — my greatest guide,
He walks with truth, without a hide.
And though the world may twist and spin,
I'll trust the paw before the grin.

"A child learns best when set free—balancing on uncertain feet, counting without charts, dreaming without limits. Let them roam, let them wonder, for freedom is the greatest teacher."

Let Them Be Free

I saw a boy on a cycle ride,
One leg slipped through the frame's side.
Holding tight, one hand on seat,
Pedalling on uncertain feet.

No guiding hand, no stern command,
Yet learning flowed—so bold, so grand.

I saw a child, barely six,
Selling lemons, quick with tricks.
Told to sell two for a five,
Yet knew how numbers come alive.

"His mother, with a knowing glance,
Measured weight without a chance,
No schooling, books, or learning charts,
Yet mastered maths with skilful art."

A fish is never taught to swim,
A monkey climbs on nature's whim.
No eagle learns from structured flight,
Yet soars with power, grace, and might.

So why must children be restrained,
Their minds controlled, their dreams contained?
Why cage the wings before they try,
Why dim the stars that light their sky?

Let them wonder, let them roam,
Let them find the world their home.
Give them space, let them explore,
Their hearts will open wisdom's door.

For those who dared to walk alone,
To carve their path, to make it known,
Became the ones the world revered—
With fearless minds and vision clear.

So let them run, let them be wild,
For every child's a learning child.
Not shaped by rules, nor bound by chains,
But free to dance in sun and rain.

The greatest gift a child can own
Is freedom's hand, to call their own.

A man with nothing but love and resolve, chiselling through an unyielding mountain—not for wealth, not for fame, but for the memory of his beloved. A tale of loss, resilience, and a path carved by sheer will.

The Mountain Man

In a hamlet high, 'neath the mountain's shade,
Lived a man, with love well laid.
Clad in *gamchha*, with toil-stained hands,
Beside him, his wife—life's golden strand.

With hearts content, no greed, no blame,
Their love was pure, their joys the same.
Then fate bestowed a gift so bright—
A life within, a child in sight.

She walked one day, through rugged land,
With food and water in her hand.
Eyes full of dreams, a mother's delight,
Yet fate had planned a tragic night.

A slip, a fall, a heart-wrenching cry,
Beneath the rocks, she lay to die.
Her husband ran—like lightning bold,
Through paths both ruthless, steep, and cold.

Two routes ahead—one smooth, yet long,
The other, fierce, but hope stayed strong.
He chose the cliffs, the jagged trail,
But time ran fast—his love turned pale.

She left too soon, her breath now gone,
His soul was crushed, yet love lived on.
Despair and sorrow, hammer in hand,
He struck the rocks, defied the land.

Not days, nor weeks, nor months, nor years,
Through scorching suns and freezing tears.
With chisel and will, he carved his way,
For those in pain, for lives to stay.

Seventy kilometres once stood tall,
Now one alone—he broke them all.
Through love and toil, the path was made,
A road of hope his hands had laid.

No crown he wore, no wealth nor fame,
Yet history glows beside his name.
Dashrath Manjhi—the Mountain Man,
Who turned despair into a plan.

And yet, we sigh at trials slight,
Lose heart when dreams drift out of sight.
But look to him, his tale so true,
A man who carved the world anew.

gamchha: a traditional thin, coarse cotton cloth used in South Asia as a towel, scarf, or loincloth.

"Two hearts, one reckless flirt—what could go wrong? A charming young man learns a hilarious lesson in love as he outruns both romance and retribution! Will he escape, or will love's laughter leave its mark forever?"

Love's Laughter – A Tale of My Younger Days

Ah, what should I say of love in old age?
Back in the day, I too took the stage.
Oh yes, my youth—though brief it did shine,
Two lovely girls had caught these eyes of mine!

The first was Tarana, a beauty so rare,
Graceful and charming beyond all compare.
But fate had a twist—oh, how unfair!
Her friend Afasana? Even lovelier, I swear!

Now, don't be fooled, I was quite a catch,
With a flirtatious heart and a game to match!
But why blame just me for love's sweet crime?
Their glances too were playful, sublime!

Had I kept it simple, all would be fine,
But greed made me dream both could be mine!
One, I dated with love so grand,
The other, I flirted with—oh, wasn't I a man?

But tables turned, as fate would play,
For Afasana was spying, keeping me at bay!
She hatched a plan, oh clever indeed,
To teach me a lesson for my misdeed!

A secret meeting in the park was set,
I grinned, thinking, "Ah! My best moment yet!"
We sat and we laughed, no worry, no care,
Until—BOOM! Tarana was suddenly there!

With fire in her eyes and sandals in hand,
I knew right then—I'd made my last stand!
Both of them charged, I ran for my life,
Dodging their wrath, escaping their strife!

Through the streets, I dashed in despair,
But fate betrayed me—oh, life's not fair!
The crowd burst in laughter, enjoying the show,
While I, poor Romeo, faced love's final blow!

Moral of the Story:

A bird in the hand is worth two in the bush,
Play smart in love, don't be in a rush! 😆

When walls close in and restless thoughts echo in despair, where do you turn for solace? A tree's shade, a river's song, or the endless horizon—somewhere beyond barriers, where the heart finds its way back to peace. A journey from turmoil to tranquility, a longing for a place beyond walls.

A Place Beyond Walls

When restless thoughts in sorrow rise,
and strike these walls before my eyes,
they turn, rebound, yet never cease,
denying my troubled mind its peace.

Oh, take me, heart, to lands so wide,
where walls don't stand, nor fears reside.
Beneath a tree, so strong, so tall,
whose shade brings calm, whose whispers call.

Or by a river, soft and deep,
where gentle waves in silence sweep,
and rising ripples, light and free,
awaken dreams long lost in me.

Upon the shore where oceans roar,
where tides retreat, then rise once more,
I'll watch them dance, I'll learn their way,
how time and fate will shift each day.

Or call the winds to race and find,
the veils that mask the truth behind,
to strip away each false disguise,
and show the world through honest eyes.

Beyond the weight of fear, beyond the chains of faith, lies a truth unspoken—one that needs no approval, no creed, no guilt. A journey unfolds, not towards heaven or hell, but towards freedom. Will you walk it?

"Beyond Fear, Beyond Faith"

They told me to bow, to kneel, to comply,
To follow the rules, but why should I?
They spoke of love, yet whispered fear,
A Father in heaven, but a judge too near.

They built their bridges with guilt and shame,
Called it faith, yet played a game.
They promised heaven, warned of hell,
But who decides? Who rings the bell?

I looked around, I looked within,
Saw the sun rise with no sin.
The river flowed, the wind was free,
No prayer was needed for them to be.

Some call themselves faithful, yet live in dread,
Counting sins, weighing words unsaid.
While those with no gods, no books to recite,
Walk unburdened, bathed in light.

Not fearing the end, not chained by decree,
They own their actions, they stand free.
No greed for heaven, no terror of flames,
Only the truth, no sacred names.

What if life is not a test,
Not a war between cursed and blessed?
What if the goal is not to atone,
But to love, to think, to be our own?

I need no middleman, no whispered creed,
No weight of rules that none can heed.
I will not fear the path ahead—
For truth is lived, not blindly read.